BUYING GOLD AND SILVER

AND OTHER PRECIOUS METALS

BY

MATTHEW CSERHATI

BUYING GOLD AND SILVER * MATTHEW CSERHATI

This book is copyrighted material.

Matthew Cserhati, 2018 ©

Second Edition, 2020.

Third Edition, 2021.

BUYING GOLD AND SILVER * MATTHEW CSERHATI

CONTENTS

WHY BUY GOLD AND SILVER?...........5

DIFFERENT KINDS OF GOLD AND SILVER..9

UNITS OF GOLD AND SILVER............12

RARE COINS..17

PURCHASING GOLD AND SILVER...19

SELLING YOUR GOLD AND SILVER 24

STORING YOUR GOLD AND SILVER 29

PRECIOUS METALS IRA 32

BUYING GOLD AND SILVER *
MATTHEW CSERHATI

"...THE BORROWER IS SERVANT TO THE LENDER." (PROVERBS 22:7)

I

WHY BUY GOLD AND SILVER?

Only about **1-3%** of the American populace owns any kind of precious metals, which include gold (Au), silver (Ag), platinum (Pd), palladium (Pd), however, experts include other elements as well. Besides being part of jewelry, these precious metals are useful because of their **physical properties**. Precious metals are used in electronics, dentistry, thermal insulation, and as catalysts and in batteries. Silver has the highest electrical and thermal conductivity of all elements, and is also used as an antimicrobial agent[1]. Thus, precious metals are a precious commodity that always has value. Furthermore, precious metals are compact and therefore easy to store.

---

[1] thoughtco.com/list-of-precious-metals-608467

BUYING GOLD AND SILVER *
MATTHEW CSERHATI

As opposed to paper money, precious metals retain their worth over long periods of history. The value of paper money may fluctuate with the stock market, and may undergo **inflation**, or hyper-inflation. Inflation is caused both by prices going up, because of increased demand for goods, and also the amount of paper money put into circulation by the **Federal Reserve Bank** (also known as the Fed)[2]. With rising prices, the dollars' worth steadily decreases. At present the monetary value of dollars in circulation is greater than the amount of precious metals that are stored in the banks.

For example, in 1923, after World War I, the US Dollar was worth 4,210,500,000,000 German Marks during the Weimar Republic[3]. Figure 1[4] shows a 50 Billion German mark from 1923. Trends also show that the worth of the US Dollar is also in decline.

---

[2] money.howstuffworks.com/how-inflation-works.htm

[3] en.wikipedia.org/wiki/Hyperinflation_in_the_Weimar_Republic

[4] tse4.mm.bing.net/th?id=OIP.ritojgbQqPagqnqWQikGWAHaD2&pid=15.1&P=0&w=295&h=154

BUYING GOLD AND SILVER * MATTHEW CSERHATI

Figure 1. Fifty Billion German Mark from 1923

Therefore, it is very useful to have some sort of stock in precious metals. If some sort of terrible calamity would occur, such as a world war, or far-reaching natural catastrophe, people would be able to start their lives over again using their stored-up amounts of gold, silver and/or other precious metals. Precious metals will always be worth a lot of money therefore, whatever the worth of the dollar or other monetary unit may be.

In fact, when paper money first began being widely used and circulated in the United States in the nineteenth century, many people resisted the use of paper money instead of metal coinage. People instinctively trusted coins because of the value of their metal as opposed to paper bills, which seemed to be worth not much more than the paper that they were printed on. Eventually paper money caught on because a large amount of it could be represented on a single bill. Paper money was said to be backed by silver or gold, meaning that the holder of the bill could exchange the bill at any time for the amount of silver or gold represented on the bill.

Precious metals were used as the original currency because they had value, as opposed to paper bills. But even metal coinage itself was used as a substitute for simply trading goods which had value, i.e. exchanging food for oil.

Nowadays bitcoin represents yet another layer of abstraction of currency beyond that of paper money: electronic currency. With our money present in online bank accounts, the chance that our money is hacked presents a new problem of this type of currency.

II

DIFFERENT KINDS OF GOLD AND SILVER

As mentioned in the previous chapter, there are many kinds of precious metals. Here we will deal with only two of these, which are by far the most well-known and also the most popular, gold and silver.

Gold is known as a yellowish, slightly soft metal. However, gold can also be reddish or whitish in color. The reason gold can be different in color if it forms alloys with other metals. White, if alloyed with silver, as in wedding rings, or reddish if alloyed with copper[5]. Figure 2[6] depicts a ternary plot of different colors of gold.

---

[5]

en.wikipedia.org/wiki/Colored_gold#Rose,_red,_and_pink_gold

[6]

upload.wikimedia.org/wikipedia/commons/thumb/e/e7/Ag-Au-Cu-colours-english.svg/350px-Ag-Au-Cu-

BUYING GOLD AND SILVER *
MATTHEW CSERHATI

The term **karat** describes the purity of gold or silver. "Pure" gold is 24 karat, with 24 being the highest karat value. The reason I say "pure" gold is because there is no such thing as a coin which is all gold, there is always some other contaminating effect. The purest of gold is 0.9999 fine gold.

Therefore, 18 karat corresponds to 75% gold (since 18/24 = 75%). Gold with lower karat values are redder in color, due to the other alloy metal showing through (usually copper). Gold rings range between 12 and 24 karats, though usually more towards lower karat values. Precious metals never occur in entirely 100% pure form, neither can they be refined to complete purity.

Silver, on the other hand can be either **pure** or **sterling**[7]. Pure, otherwise known as sterling silver is 99.9% silver. Sterling silver is something akin to gold of lower karat values, and is made up of only 92.5% silver, alloyed with 7.5% copper.

---

colours-english.svg.png
[7] https://www.jewelrynotes.com/sterling-silver-vs-pure-silver-what-is-the-difference/

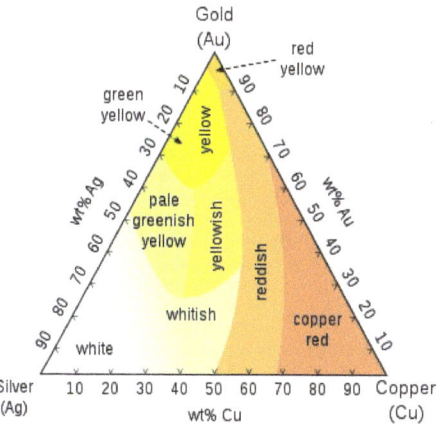

Figure 2. Ternary plot of different gold-silver-copper alloys

Gold and silver can be counterfeited; therefore, it is important to be able to tell fake gold from true gold. Gold is not magnetic, but silver is slightly magnetic. A good way to tell if a metal is gold or silver is if you slide it down a surface at an angle with a magnet beneath it (such as a small neodymium or praseodymium magnet). Gold will slide right down, silver will slide down a little slowly.

III

UNITS OF GOLD AND SILVER

Gold and silver take several forms. They can be in the form of coins and bars (also known as bullion or ingots) of different shapes and sizes, different purities, and different mints (different engravings). Gold and silver are also measured in grams, kilograms, ounces, Troy ounces, and pounds. Most often, gold and silver are measured in **Troy ounces**.

The Troy ounce is a unit of weight similar to a regular ounce. Its usage can be traced back to the fourteenth century to the Troyes market in France, and which was adapted by King Henry II in England during his reign. One troy ounce is actually heavier than a regular ounce by a factor of 1.09714. Thus, one ounce of material is equivalent to 0.911458 Troy ounces. Furthermore, 12

Troy ounces make up a Troy pound, whereas 16 ounces make up a regular pound[8]. From this we can see that a Troy pound is actually lighter than a regular pound.

Gold and silver coins can come in forms of 1 oz., ¼ oz. and 1/10 oz, each representing decreasing values. Gold and silver can come in smaller or larger (and heavier) sized bars.

An important term in buying and trading with gold is the **spot**. The spot is basically nothing more than any kind of unit of precious metal. Therefore, five gold ¼ oz. coins are five spots. Seventeen silver 1 oz. coins represent 17 spots, and so on and so forth. Prices for precious metals are given for their one-ounce spot. So, for example, on September 29, 2018, gold spot (that is, 1 ounce of gold, coin or any other form) was worth $1,195.00.

Gold and silver coins are made by different mints all across the world. The five most well-known ones are:

- The United States Mint

---

[8] jmbullion.com/investing-guide/types-physical-metals/troy-oz

- The Royal Canadian Mint
- The Perth Mint (Australia)
- PAMP Suisse (Switzerland)
- Sunshine Mint (USA)

It is important to note that a coin which was not produced by these mints is most likely a counterfeit. Also, a silver coin must also have the inscription **"Troy ounce"**, and also **"999 FINE SILVER"**, *otherwise it is most likely a fake*. Similarly, a gold coin must have the inscription **"FINE GOLD"** on it.

Figure 3. Front and back sides of an American Eagle and a Silver Buffalo.[9]

---

[9] apmex.com

BUYING GOLD AND SILVER * MATTHEW CSERHATI

A common type of gold coin is the **American Eagle** gold coin, and a common type of silver coin is the 1 oz. **Silver Buffalo**. Samples of these coins can be seen in Figure 3 above. Certain versions of the Buffalo coin have a circle in the middle, which if you place a certain type of optical lens over it, the word 'VALID' becomes visible. This is used to protect against counterfeiting the coin.

From the Royal Canadian Mint, we have the **Canadian Maple Leaf** coin, which is common. It has a picture of Queen Elizabeth II on the flipside.

The **Austrian Philharmonic** gold coin is also a common type of gold coin of European mintage. It is also present in one-half and one-quarter denominations. It is also available in silver bullion, just as the American Buffalo is also available in gold as well.

Swiss **20 Franc Helvetia** coins are also common. They are smaller in size and weight, containing 0.1867 oz of gold. They are good to purchase if you don't have money for a whole one-ounce coin.

BUYING GOLD AND SILVER *
MATTHEW CSERHATI

Coins are also available in platinum as well, but with only a smaller number of denominations than gold and silver. Platinum Maple Leafs are one kind of platinum coin that are available.

Sometimes gold rings are measured in grams (g), gold and silver bars are also measured in kilograms (kg). One kg is equal to 1,000 g. One Troy oz. of metal is equal to 31.1035 g, 1 oz. of metal is worth 28.3495 g of material. Therefore, for example, if 1 Troy oz. of gold is $1,195, then 100 g (3.21507 Troy oz.) of gold is worth $3,842.

IV

RARE COINS

Another commodity that coin traders deal with are rare coins. These coins have value because of their rarity, age and historical value. They can be worth several hundreds or even thousands of dollars.

Some coins are also are, because they have errors in them, compared to normally minted coins. Such errors include missing dates or inscriptions, or have been misprinted. A list of error coins can be found at coins.thefuntimesguide.com/us-error-coins-list together with their prices.

Many rare coins include pennies, nickels, dimes, quarters, half dollars and dollar coins, which do not contain much silver in them. The gold and silver content of these coins is much less than coins made of pure silver or pure gold. However, there are silver and gold coins with a high purity that are worth more than their weight because of their antiquity. However, their value goes down the more worn they are. A coin which has hardly been circulated and hasn't been worn down due to many people touching it is worth much more than a coin which has barely legible inscriptions. Following is one of several scales that numismatic professionals use to grade coins based on their wear and tear. It has a scale from 1-70[10]:

Scale	Grading
1	Poor
2	Fair
3	About good
4–6	Good
8–10	Very good
12–15	Fine
20–35	Very fine
40–45	Extremely fine
50–58	About uncirculated
60–62	Uncirculated
63	Select uncirculated
64	Choice uncirculated
65–66	Gem uncirculated
67–69	Superb gem uncirculated
70	Perfect uncirculated

[10] coins.ha.com/tutorial/coin-grading.s

V

PURCHASING GOLD AND SILVER

Gold and silver can be purchased at a local coin store, or they can be ordered over the Internet (which choice may be more expensive). Three well-known online precious metal resources are APMEX (apmex.com), JM BULLION (jmbullion.com) and KITCO (online.kitco.com). These websites also have useful detailed information on buying and selling gold and silver.

As mentioned previously, gold and silver are sold at a rate above **spot prices**. The spot price of a given precious metal is its worth in dollars when the miners dig it out of the ground. The metals must then be cleaned, processed, refined, and turned into coins in order to be sold in stores. Metal bars cost less because they do not need to be turned into coins, and also because of their higher mass, they sell for an overall smaller price. The prices of gold, silver and other precious metals is reported on the APMEX, JM BULLION and KITCO websites, and changes multiple times a day, somewhat like the stock market. Therefore, it is worth checking up on spot prices regularly, at least every one or two days. For example, gold spot was worth $1,195.54, and silver spot was worth $14.72 according to the JM BULLION website. Figure 4 depicts the change in spot price of gold over the past six months.

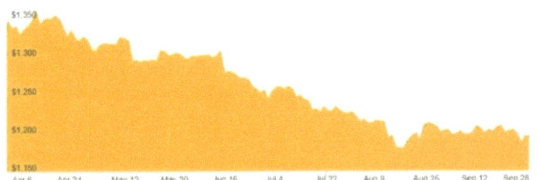

Figure 4. Changes in gold spot price between April 1 and September 29, 2018 according to the APMEX website.

Gold and silver prices follow each other's upturns and downturns. One other long-term general trend is that the relative worth of gold is getting higher and higher compared to that of silver. As an illustration, to date, a single 1/10 oz. gold coin is roughly equal to eight 1 oz. silver coins in price.

For the most part gold and silver prices are stable, although they can change due to certain events. Gold and silver prices tend to rise when there is uncertainty and instability concerning current events, and conversely, prices tend to decrease when things are more stable. For example, in Figure 5 we can see that gold prices dropped around the time of the 2016 presidential elections. Also, gold and silver prices rose about 50% during the covid19 pandemic. There has hardly been a time after February of 2020 when gold prices were below $1,550 per ounce. As per the writing of the third edition of this book, in some precious metal stores they have run out of smaller denominations of gold coins.

Therefore, naturally, it is wisest to buy gold and silver when the prices are low, and sell when the prices are high. That is why it is important to check spot prices to note general trends, and to anticipate spot price changes when following current political and/or social trends. Since we are all sinners, the people who set spot prices may not be uninfluenced by political leanings or other factors.[11]

It is also important to note that when buying gold or silver spot, the sellers may add an extra 10-15% to the spot price, since they want to make a profit. Therefore, if I want to buy 1 oz. of gold spot, and if the price of gold spot is $1,1195, then the *actual purchasing price* is $1,374.25. If you buy gold or silver spot in higher quantities (i.e. if you buy 20 1

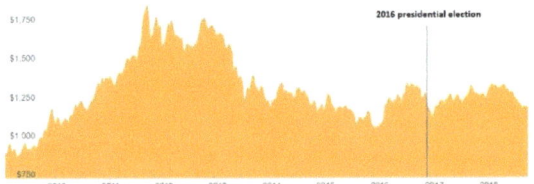

Figure 5. Gold spot prices between January 20, 2009 and September 29, 2018

oz. coins), then the sellers might give you a discount for higher quantities. Buying more of smaller denominations is more advantageous than less of larger denominations, even though they may amount to the same price. For example, if I

---

[11] "For the love of money is a root of all kinds of evil..." (1Timothy 6:10)

BUYING GOLD AND SILVER * MATTHEW CSERHATI

buy two 1 oz. gold coins at $1,1195/spot, the total price comes up to 2 x 1195 x 1.15 = $2,748.50, at 15% per spot. If I buy 20 1/10 oz. coins, however, for 10% extra per spot (bulk cost), this amounts to 20 x (1195 / 10) x 1.10 = $2,629.00, which is a difference of $119.50.

Always purchase gold and silver at respected local dealers. Ask your friends as to which store has a good reputation. Check online testimonies or look up the store at the Better Business Bureau. When buying, always ask for a full receipt with details about the purchase (i.e. how much of which denomination, spot price, etc.).

VI

SELLING YOUR GOLD AND SILVER

Buying gold and silver is one thing, but selling it is another. Obviously, when prices get high, due to political events and/or other circumstances, you might have the chance to make money by selling your precious metals. Gold and silver coin shops will purchase your precious metals from you.

Obviously, you want to make a profit off of your precious metals when selling them. Now, just as when coin sellers sell you gold and silver, they add an extra 10–15% onto the spot price to make a profit, they will also buy your precious metals at less than full price. This means that the price of precious metals has to really increase between the time you bought your precious metals and the time when you sell them.

Also beware that some coin stores may buy precious metals from you at different rates, based on whatever online resource they are following. For example, at 2:00 PM on July 29, 2020, the buying price of 1 oz. of gold at APMEX was $1,967.60, whereas on KITCO it was $1,946.00. Obviously then, coin dealers will buy at the lowest online rates to save more money.

This just highlights the practical necessity of teaming up with other individuals who buy and sell precious metals. Don't act alone. Ask for advice. Buy when others buy, and sell when others sell. If you are buying when no-one else is doing so, you might be making a mistake. According to a wise Hungarian saying, "more eyes see more things". The Bible says "In the multitude of counselors there is safety." (Proverbs 11:14)

For example, coin sellers will pay 95% of the spot price for an American Eagle coin, and 93% of spot price for a Gold Prospector coin (see figure 6). So that means that if the spot price for 1 oz. of gold is $1500, then the sellers will pay you only $1500 x 0.95 = $1425 for the American

Eagle, and only $1500 x 0.93 = $1395 for the Gold Prospector coin. For the Gold Prospector coin that's more than $100 less than spot price! Obviously, selling and buying coins is a lucrative business.

Figure 6. 1986 Engelhard Gold Prospector 1/10 oz coin.[12]

Let's take a real-life example. The date of the writing of the second edition of this book is now July 21, 2020. There is unrest in the big cities, it's four months before the election, and the covid19 virus is affecting many people's lives.[13] Therefore, gold spot price is high. It is $1,835.80 on the present day. I bought several gold ¼ oz. American

---

[12] montanararities.com/engelhard-gold-prospector-tenth-oz.html

[13] Indeed, at the onset of the covid19 virus in America many people were buying up gold and silver coins even at higher prices. Precious metals were hard to come buy.

BUYING GOLD AND SILVER * MATTHEW CSERHATI

Eagle coins at a spot price of around $1,250, at 15% above spot price. What would be my profit if I sold one of these ¼ oz. coins?

Let's do the math then! The spot price for one ¼ oz. American Eagle is 0.25 x $1,250 = $312.50. We have to multiply this by 15%, which means that the buying price for the coin is 1.15 x $312.50 = **$359.38**. If I want to sell this coin at a spot price of $1,835.80, this corresponds to 0.25 x $1,835.80 = $458.95. But, since the coin trader buys it for only 95% of spot price, you will make 0.95 x $458.95 = **$436.00** from selling the coin. This makes for a profit of $436.00 − $359.38 = $76.62.

That's quite a nice deal for a single ¼ oz. coin. The secret of buying and selling gold and silver is that you have to buy and sell in bulk. If you could sell 100 of these ¼ oz. coins, we'd be talking about a profit of around $7,600. Buying and selling precious metals is obviously a long-term project, where you must carefully watch how prices fluctuate so that you know when to buy and sell.

BUYING GOLD AND SILVER *
MATTHEW CSERHATI

In general, you can calculate the profit that you'd make by selling your coin with the following equation:

$$profit = f \cdot (b \cdot p(sell) - a \cdot p(buy))$$

where p(sell) is the selling spot price, p(buy) is the buying spot price, b is the proportion of the full price that that the coin trader will buy the coin for (i.e. 96% for an American Eagle), and a is the proportion of the spot price that the trader will sell you the coin for (i.e. 115%). The parameter f is the fraction of 1 oz. coin. For example, for a ¼ oz. coin, f = 0.25, for a 1/10 oz. coin, it is 0.1.

VII

STORING YOUR GOLD AND SILVER

Usually, your seller will give you your coins in small plastic pouches for individual coins. Once you have purchased gold or silver, you must store them in a safe place. Multiple gold and silver coins are usually stored in plastic tubes.

Store your gold and silver in a safe. Safes come as cheap as $50. Safes differ in size, as well as the maximum temperature that they can withstand, as well as the amount of time that the safe can be exposed to a fire before the contents of the safe start getting damaged.

The shortest fire time limit is about 45 minutes for the cheapest safes. This means that your precious metals will start melting 45 minutes after the fire starts. However, if your precious metals do melt, they are not entirely lost. Their worth only decreases a little, because they were melted, but are still worth a lot.

Figure 7. Plastic tubes for storing coins.14

Safes can be purchased at large stores such as Walmart or at locksmith shops. Always make sure to make a copy of the key as well.

Fortunately, gold does not rust or tarnish, since gold is the least reactive of all of the elements. It does not even react with oxygen, which is the most reactive of all elements. On the other hand, sterling silver may tarnish if it comes in contact with perspiration which has a high enough

---

14 rrbi.co/2020-tube-of-20-silver-eagles

concentration of salt. Pure silver does not tarnish, since it does not react with water or oxygen. It may tarnish however with wear and tear[15].

---

[15] onecklace.com/tips/why-does-silver-tarnish/

VIII

PRECIOUS METALS IRA

Besides regular Individual Retirement Accounts (IRA), with precious metals, there is also a possibility to open an IRA backed by precious metals. This is useful, since as we stated earlier, the value of the dollar may fluctuate, but gold and other precious metals have kept their value over history.

What exactly does this mean? Just like a normal IRA, with your job provider, you can open a precious metals IRA by paying into it a certain amount of money. Different companies require a certain amount of money to start up this kind of IRA. The higher quality ones, such as Birch Gold or Hartford Gold require that you put down at least $25,000 to start the IRA. You can do this by either paying cash, or with a rollover from an existing IRA account. After certain amounts (like $100,000) they may even offer a free amount of silver. Other companies may not require an amount.

However, application fees, annual storage fees and/or deposit fees of $25-$100 may apply. A list of precious metals IRA companies can be seen below.

Company	Website
Hartford Gold	americanhartfordgold.com
Birch Gold	birchgold.com
The Entrust Group	theentrustgroup.com
Goldstar Trust	goldstarttrust.com
Kingdom Trust Company	kingdomtrust.com
STRATA Trust Company	stratatrust.com
Equity Institutional	equityinstitutional.com

The way a precious metals IRA works is that you can withdraw the money in the IRA in gold or any other precious metal, or you can liquidate it in the form of cash. The value of the gold in the account fluctuates with the price of gold on the market. You can also pay into your account at any time to increase its value.

The advantages of a precious metals, IRA is that it is convenient. You can withdraw money from it at any time, like a bank account. Furthermore, the company stores your physical metals for you, so you don't have to be in fear that somebody will steal it from you. Furthermore, company representatives can help you with professional help regarding your IRA.

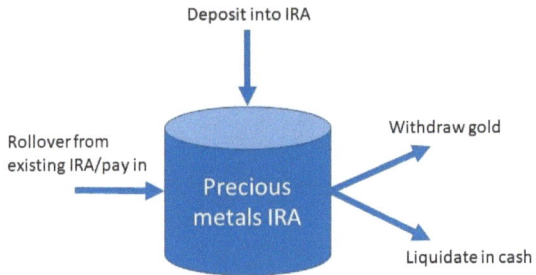

Figure 8. The concept of a precious metals IRA.

However, the disadvantages are the fees you have to pay. For example, many companies purchase the precious metals from APMEX, which can be a little pricy.

BUYING GOLD AND SILVER *
MATTHEW CSERHATI

NOTES

BUYING GOLD AND SILVER *
MATTHEW CSERHATI

NOTES